D1522021

God Is Calling

When you seek me with
all your heart, you will find me.
Jeremiah 29:13

To Alexandre, my cousin

Under the direction of Romain Lizé, CEO, MAGNIFICAT
Editor, MAGNIFICAT: Isabelle Galmiche
Editor, Ignatius: Vivian Dudro
Traductor: Janet Chevrier
Artistic Designers: Armelle Riva, Gauthier Delauné
Production: Thierry Dubus, Audrey Bord

Original French edition: *Cherche Dieu de tout ton cœur*
© Mame, Paris, 2021
ISBN MAGNIFICAT 978-1-949239-94-2 • ISBN Ignatius Press 978-1-62164-570-2

Brother François Fontanié, C.F.R.

God Is Calling

Seeing His Signs in Your Life

MAGNIFICAT · Ignatius

Contents

"Francis, why was this church built?"

"Over the centuries, God has left signs of his presence in the lives of men and women. And they responded by building this church."

"Did God leave signs in your life too?"

God left a sign
of his presence in my life through
the example of the saints.

When I was little, my mother taught me about many saints. I was amazed by their heroic lives.

It was as though a common light shone through these men and women.

That light was the light of God.

God left a sign
of his presence in my life
through the example of
the religious brothers
and sisters around me.

Look how Sister Catherine loves the poor...

See the happiness of Brother Anthony...

What is the source of their joy and their service?

3

God left a sign
of his presence in my life
through his creation.

As a child, I spent hours observing nature.

Look at the light shimmering through the leaves, at the grace of that bird taking flight; see the noble look of that deer...

It's as though all that lives and breathes were singing the praises of a mysterious Creator.

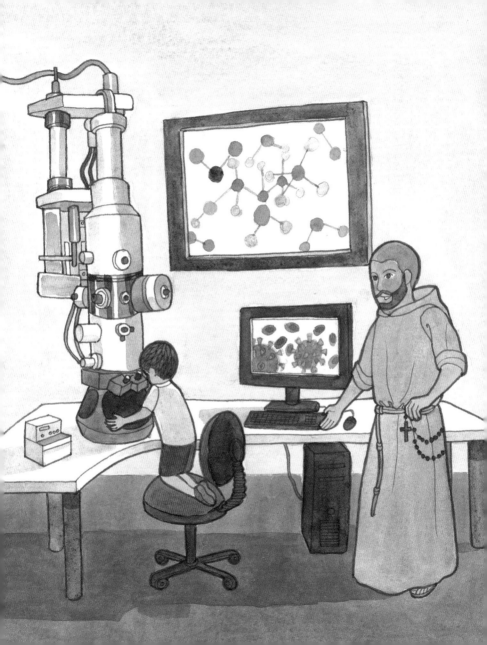

As I grew up, I studied science. I soon realized there's no end to our learning about the universe.

Since discovering the tiny cell, we have gone on to discover things even smaller.

Since discovering the large planets, we have gone on to discover objects in space that are even bigger.

And everything, from the very small to the very big, is so beautiful!

Could all of that really have happened by accident?

4

God left a sign
of his presence in my life
through the Bible.

As a young man, I started to read the Bible.

I'm still reading it today and still mining its treasures.

The Bible teaches us that, for millennia, men have journeyed along the same path.

That path, made most evident in the life of Jesus, goes by way of the cross and leads to resurrection and eternal life with God.

Along that path, the Bible is the Word of God. And Jesus is the Word of God made man. At each crossroad, the Word shows you which direction to take.

5

God left a sign
of his presence in my life
through providence.

One summer, I went for a trek in the south of France.

At the end of my final hike, I looked for the train station.

It was Sunday, and I had to be back in Paris for work the next day,

But there was no train station in sight anywhere!

Night was falling, and I didn't know where else to look.

On a wing and a prayer, I started to look for a ride.

And, by some miracle, I made it back to Paris in record time.

That day, I understood that divine providence isn't make-believe. God comes to our aid when we place our trust in him.

· 6 ·

God left a sign
of his presence in my life
through my *vocation.*

I truly saw a sign of God in my life when I discovered that God had a plan for me.

I had finished my studies, and I was trying to figure out what to do with my life. At Midnight Mass on Christmas Eve, I asked God: "What do you wish me to become?"

That's when I heard a small voice inside me answering: "A Franciscan in the Bronx."

A Franciscan in the Bronx? In New York City? That wasn't exactly what I'd had in mind! So I said to God, "All right, but first I need an explanation!"

Over the next five years, I went on figuring it out. I met the poor, and, little by little, the poor molded in me the heart of Saint Francis.

After five years, I paid a visit to the Franciscans, the followers of Saint Francis, in the Bronx.

It was while listening to one of them preach that I finally understood: that voice on Christmas Eve had told me the truth. My place was there.

I knew that God loved me, and I followed him.

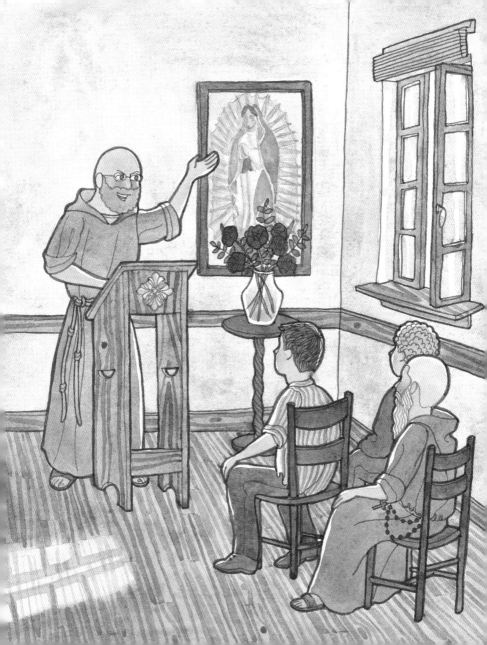

God left a sign of his presence in my life through *prayer*.

A couple of years before becoming a Franciscan, I withdrew to the silence of a monastery for a few days.

And, in the silence, God spoke to me.

Back in my cell, I took a book at random from the bookshelf. It told the story of Saint Francis kissing a leper, and it was written by a Franciscan from the Bronx.

Once again, God was showing me the way.

Then I took the habit
of Saint Francis.

Epilogue

If you, too, would like to see the signs of God in your life, say this little prayer:

"My God, if you are there, let me recognize your presence."

He who knit you in your mother's womb looks upon you with love, and he will answer you.

Printed in December 2021 by Dimograf, Poland.
Job number MGN 22003
Printed in compliance with the Consumer
Protection Safety Act, 2008